Circle
of
Giving

Donors' Stories
of Wisdom

By Janet K. Ginn, CFRE

Eudora
Press, LLC

SECOND EDITION

www.heiferfoundation.org

Publisher:
Eudora Press, LLC
P. O. Box 727
Little Rock, AR 72203

Cover:
Art Direction: Robyn R. Friday
Design: Paul Gormont

Book design, typography and typesetting by:
Paul Gormont, Apertures, Incorporated.

First Edition
ISBN 978-09785142-0-4

"For the donors I have had the privilege to know and who have welcomed me into their lives. I am inspired by your sense of service and selfless giving to change a world in need – the results of which will live on far beyond your lifetime. It is my honor to know you and assist you in making a difference in the world. May you find us faithful."

Acknowledgments

I'd like to offer my deep gratitude to my husband Randy who has shared my passion for service and has given me the freedom to serve. With his commitment, love, encouragement, and support, I am able to share this book with you. To my daughters Shannon and Marsha who have sacrificed for others they will never meet. To Greg Spradlin and Corrine Gormont who have supported me throughout this project and share my passion for making a difference in the lives of donors and recipients. To Jo Luck, my mentor and friend, for her support, faith, and encouragement for so many years. To the Heifer Foundation Board of Trustees and the Heifer Foundation staff for their faith, trust, courage, and daily support. To Charlie Owen, my attorney and friend, for his keen insight and encouragement. And to the wonderful Heifer donors and recipients who have so freely shared their lives with me and have become compelling figures who inspire so many to strive to be better by sharing their values to make our world a better place. Without these this book would not have been possible.

And, finally, to all who have gone on before us who have entrusted us to pass on their values and valuables, may they find us faithful!

Foreword

While writing this book I found myself drawn to the image of a circle. It's a wondrous thing, the circle, with its dependable shape and undetectable beginning and ending. It reminds me of the intimate, continuous connection between generous donors and people in need. If a circle were a living thing, it would be self-sustaining, wise, and endless, like the relationships that are created with a single gift.

Throughout my many years of service to individuals and families devoted to ending world hunger, I've witnessed how a charitable gift begins a unique circle of hope and success—a circle that profoundly changes the lives of donors and their families as much as the lives of recipients and their communities. A remarkable thing happens as a result of a gift. The newly formed circle grows and continues to feed all of its members—donors and recipients—and the future generations of both.

I'm writing this book to honor these circles and to help caring people like you make a greater impact on the future of the world. By taking good care of yourself and your loved ones, you can take better care of those in need.

As president and CEO of Heifer Foundation, I have the wonderful opportunity to work daily with inspiring, selfless individuals of every age and every walk of life. Most have become cherished friends. All have taught me life lessons. I have been honored to help each of them find their way through the process of choosing the right instruments to plan their financial futures in order to fulfill their dreams of helping others.

While this book focuses on my personal experiences at Heifer Foundation and those of the donors I have worked closely with to end world hunger, it is my hope that as you read, you are inspired to create a legacy that reflects your values and meets your personal calling and desires. Whether you wish to join me in ending world hunger through Heifer's unique mission of sustainability or you want to focus your resources on another worthy cause, we all share the same belief that we can change a world in need.

And our world is in great need. It is devastated by war and disease. We live on a planet that is struggling to create the necessary materials to sustain life. In once fertile lands, water no longer flows and deserts are taking over. Today more than eight hundred million people go to bed hungry every night and about 24,000 people die every day because of malnutrition and related diseases. Three-

---

[1] State of Food Insecurity in the World 2005. Food and Agriculture Organization of the United Nations.

fourths of these deaths are children under the age of five. That is approximately one child every five seconds.[1]

Yet there is great hope. Together, we can do so much. All across the world inspired individuals are supporting the efforts of their beloved charitable organizations. I am heartened to hear that according to the United Nations Development Program, the basic health and nutrition needs of the world's poorest people could be met for an additional $13 billion a year. While this is no small sum, it is within our reach. Think of how much we spend as a society to create major motion pictures, or to feed our pets, or to buy beautiful gifts our children and grandchildren will outgrow. We *can* eliminate the global burden of hunger and poverty by providing families and communities the means to feed themselves. I have personally seen water buffalo make the difference of life and death to families in Asia. I've met a young girl and heard her story of how a goat enabled her family in Uganda to purchase clothes and send her to school.

As you begin to consider how you want to change the world and investigate the organizations that share your values and goals, bear in mind that your role as a donor is critical. You represent the life force of a giving circle.

There is a proverb that says: "Tell me and I will probably forget. Show me and I might remember. Involve me and I will never forget."

Many donors come to Heifer Foundation because they have been involved in, or moved by, Heifer International's unique mission to solve world hunger by providing a sustainable means of self-reliance to those in need. While part of Heifer Foundation's mission is to generate ongoing support for the work of Heifer International, our focus remains firmly on our donors. We are focused on the values and valuables you want to pass on to future generations. Who in your family, or circle of friends, needs your support? How can you create a legacy that reflects the way you live your life? What can you do to protect your assets so that you will be able to support yourself *and* a world in need?

No matter what cause fulfills your philanthropic goals, *you* must come first. By understanding planned charitable giving instruments, such as bequests, annuities, trusts, and endowments—and the charities that provide them—you can create a plan with the help of your advisors that ensures financial peace for your future first and then for the future of others.

How can you help others if you are without resources? Have you considered whether your retirement plan will provide enough income should you live beyond your 90's? Have you wondered what might happen to your home if you require unexpected medical care in your golden years? Do you know how you can be sure that your special-needs child will be provided for financially when you're gone?

It has always been my job, and my honor, to guarantee that donors and their desires come first. Wouldn't it be wonderful to lead an independent life until the end; leave a loving gift to your children, grandchildren, place of worship, and community program; and also begin a sustaining circle that changes the lives of suffering people in a community or country of your choice? Wouldn't it be wonderful to honor parents or special relationships with an endowment that reflects the values that they've bestowed on you? Wouldn't it be wonderful to invest in one or more initiatives—like protecting the earth's dwindling resources or helping youth at risk the world over—and watch your investment grow over the years?

You must always come first. You know what's important to you. You must decide how the allocation of your wealth, during your life and afterward, represents who you are.

As I travel around the country giving informational seminars and spending wonderful days visiting with loving people devoted to helping others, I'm often asked why I'm so driven to educate donors. Helping the hungry is obvious, yes. But why this passion for donors? Here is my answer.

I was very close to a woman who, with her husband,

raised five children on a 2,000-acre farm that I'm sure was modeled after the Garden of Eden. The smell of the grass alone after a heavy rain was pure heaven. Add the tall oaks with children's initials carved in the bark, and the creak of the screen door against a chorus of blue jays in the back yard, and you couldn't imagine a more perfect setting for comfort. And this wasn't a Hollywood set. It was a real farm in Arkansas.

That woman was dear to me. She taught me how to serve others and that the glass is always half full, not half empty. She was also dear to the school children she decided to cook for when she turned 50. She brought eggs from her own hens and fresh milk from her cows to school every morning, and after she made sure the children had enough food for their bones and their brains, she'd pack up bundles to send home to the rest of their families. She could call them all by their first names. She asked about siblings and parents. She did this for 20 years.

She decided to retire in her 70s. She devoted her time to gardening, which she loved, and cooking for her husband who loved fresh fish from his stocked ponds. They lived the kind of life most of us only vaguely remember from our childhoods or from our parents' stories – a life full of hard work, but also full of lazy evenings with crossword puzzles and a fire in the fireplace.

Her husband of 60 years passed away when she was

76. She continued to live in her house of 60 years, but began to sell off property to maintain an income to pay for taxes from the sale of the land, to pay for care after a stroke, to purchase groceries and make long-distance phone calls to grandchildren, to keep a nurse after her second stroke, and so on. Through all of this, she often talked about those school children and her desire to help children all around the world.

In the end, all of her property was gone. The farmhouse was sold to pay for her care when she was 92 years old. She lived her remaining seven years in a nursing home, subsidized by her family and government programs. On her bedside table, she kept a photo of herself and her husband. That photo of them standing proudly in front of the house with the creaky screen door was all that was left of the life they built together.

Sometimes when I'm driving to meet a potential donor across a winding back road with the windows rolled down, I get a familiar whiff of grass that reminds me of that slice of heaven in Arkansas and what I feel I'm here on earth to do.

If I had known then what I know now, this precious woman's farm could have provided more than enough to ensure an independent, comfortable life in the house she loved until the end. She could have passed on an inheritance to her beloved children, as well as create a lasting circle for giving to children all around the world.

What I know now can still help. It can help you plan for your future. One that is dignified, comfortable, and a reflection of how you live your life.

This book is part of my legacy, and a tribute to the many inspiring donors whose stories are included. It is organized so that you can easily jump around and assimilate the more "technical" information and enjoy the donor stories in a way that makes sense for you.

My hope is that while you read others' stories, review our sample calculations, and begin to better understand what planned charitable giving instruments can do for you and those in need, you will take the time to reflect on your own values and what you want your wealth to say about your life. It is a striking statistic that seven out of ten people die without a will. I know it's hard to think of a world without us in it; our life's work coming to an end. Over the years, I've worked with people who have had to face very difficult decisions. Who's going to get the old homestead? How can I say goodbye to a business that I built over 50 years? How will my children feel about my plan to give to charity? What if I have been touched by a number of charities and want to give back to all of them? And so on. These, of course, are questions only you can answer for yourself. The duty of leaders of charitable organizations is to understand your wishes and carry them out. Whatever you struggle with while making your plan, however, I can tell you that the magic of beginning a circle of giving is indisputable, as you will find in our donors' stories. As you read through this book and begin to think about your options and your passions, you will know the right path to take because your heart will be at peace, and looking into the future will be a joy.

Contents

Section I

Opening Your
Heart to a
World in Need

Introduction

Anyone who has ever fallen in love knows the feeling of sudden and complete vulnerability. Each time I delivered my two daughters, I fell in love. I felt overwhelming joy and gratitude mixed with a new fear. If anything were to happen to my girls, I would be devastated. How could I protect them?

Of course, every parent's wish is to protect his or her children – to raise them to fulfill their dreams, prosper, and live healthy and happy lives.

In 1996, I witnessed mothers, in love just like me, struggle to raise their children. But unlike me, these mothers were struggling to put food on their tables. Education was a luxury. Work was a luxury. Warm clothes and housing were luxuries. Mothers and fathers in Asia and Africa, Central and South America, and even in the hills of Kentucky, so close to my own home in Arkansas, were selflessly skipping meals, days at a time, so their children could eat mere morsels. They were walking miles for water that was contaminated. They were living in rain-drenched huts and using plastic bags as cover. They were without opportunities, choices, and hope. Every Sunday, at 7:30 in the morning, while my two healthy girls slept in their warm flannels under clean, quilted comforters, I watched a television program that brought the realities of hunger and poverty into my home and into my heart. I knew that without the help from caring individuals and dedicated charities, these parents would surely watch their families suffer unimaginably.

Whether we donate money or participate in charity work out of a sense of responsibility, or simply because it feels right, our hearts are always involved. A story, a cause, or a charity's mission personally touches us, and then we open our hearts to others. Few experiences give us the same joy as we receive from helping others. Ask yourself what moments have been most significant in your life, and chances are, they are the moments that you've given of yourself. The motivation to help others is one of the most important characteristics that distinguish us as humans.

After watching this particular TV program about hunger and poverty every Sunday morning for two years, I knew that working to help end world hunger was what I wanted to do with my life. But how? I learned that a variety of charities provide immediate relief from hunger with supplies of canned goods and bottled water, but it was Heifer International's unique message of self-reliance and empowerment that touched me most deeply.

Imagine the impact a daily supply of milk can make to a family who has nothing. Then imagine the impact that a weekly income from the sale of milk can have on that same family and their community. Finally, imagine that family being capable of passing on a food- and income-producing animal to a neighbor. This is the true magic of Heifer. By giving a life-sustaining animal through Heifer International, you are giving a family a permanent victory over hunger, poverty, and environmental degradation. You are creating a unique circle of giving, because every recipient of your gift also becomes a donor to another in need. Families are protected, communities thrive, and the circle of giving continues.

When I learned about the opportunity to work with Heifer Foundation, I knew that my dreams were about to come true. Not only would I finally have the opportunity to help end world hunger, I would also be able to help potential donors fulfill their dreams of making a lasting difference. I would help people like you plan a secure future for yourself and your loved ones while leaving a legacy of love to the rest of the world.

Chapter 1

Choosing Your Charity

I was impassioned inexplicably by watching hungry families struggle. Why ending world hunger is my calling as opposed to another worthy cause is unknown, but once a heart is moved by a specific cause, it is with great faith and trust that we commit ourselves to the work of one or more charities.

Charities represent the key to a better world. What they stand for, how they operate, and who they help *must* match what's in your own heart in order to gain your faith and trust, and once that happens, together you can move mountains.

Is it a coincidence that I work for a world hunger organization? Certainly not! The work of Heifer International touched the place in my heart that not only wanted to feed starving people every single day, it reached the place in my heart that was desperate to permanently change the futures of poverty-stricken families.

What is your innermost desire?

The Passion Behind Charities

While I watched loving people provide non-perishable items to bone-thin people with swollen bellies and dark circles under their eyes every Sunday morning, I suffered from a nagging anxiety. How many cans of food does it take to feed a family of four for a lifetime? What happens when the supplies run out?

People do need immediate relief from the suffering of hunger. Right this second, the physical pain and hopelessness of hunger is debilitating. But Dan West, a remarkable Midwestern farmer and founder of Heifer knew that once fed, people would still need a way to build a future. They would need opportunities, choices and training to live out a life of self-reliance. That was the message that spoke directly to my heart, and his story still moves me to tears.

In the late 1930s, Dan West went to Europe as part of a relief team and witnessed first hand the devastation of war. The Spanish Civil War had ravaged the country of Spain, obliterated food sources, eliminated jobs, and left people without the means to survive. Every day was a battle between life and death.

Dan's job as a relief worker was to provide daily rations of powdered milk to refugees—men, women, and children so hungry and traumatized by war and poverty, that they moved as if under an impossible weight, as if they were decades older than they were. Every day, Dan ladled out powdered milk to people who would otherwise have nothing to live on.

As the months passed, he began to notice a wonderful transformation, small at first — a subtle smile, a quick thank you. But soon the children began to laugh and play with sticks. They teased and hung on tree limbs and kicked rocks between what was left of their houses. They acted like children are meant to act. The protein and vitamins from the milk was strengthening their bones and providing their first glimmer of hope in a very long time. This observation gave Dan a vision for how to change the world.

When he returned to Indiana, Dan shared his vision with his wife Lucy and their then four children. *"Not a cup, but a cow."* Dan knew that the relief worker's supply of powdered milk would eventually run out, but a cow would provide the refugees with a lasting source of milk, income, and dignity.

With that one brilliant idea, and endless evangelizing to neighbors and community and church leaders, Dan founded Heifers for Relief—today, Heifer International—a nonprofit organization that provides livestock and training in animal husbandry and farming and requires all recipients to "pass on the gift" by giving away some of the offspring of their animals to others in need in their communities.

All charities begin with an amazing passion and vision. Each charity's story reflects the goodness and power in all of us. When you choose to support a charity, it is as if you are personally shaking the hand of its founder and rolling up your sleeves to work side-by-side with him or her.

Since its humble beginnings in 1944, Heifer's unique approach to hunger and poverty has assisted more than seven million families in more than 125 countries around the world out of poverty. And the numbers grow daily. But Heifer International is not about animals. It never was, and this is what continues to inspire me and fill my heart with joy.

Heifer International's projects respond aggressively to gender inequity, violence, natural disasters, the degradation of natural resources, and devastating trends such as the spread of HIV/AIDS. Heifer International also provides education programs that explore global issues of poverty and hunger while challenging all of us to become more responsible global citizens. Dan West's vision was to change the world, and indeed, he has. The requirement that recipients of Heifer animals pass on some of their animals' offspring to other needy families within their community keeps the circle of giving alive for generations. It provides hope to entire communities and turns every recipient into a donor like you and me. Your family shares its wealth with a needy family miles and miles away. That family passes on their "wealth" of an animal's offspring to another family, who does the same, and on and on the circle lives and grows.

CHANGING THE WORLD

A number of charitable organizations offer special programs where you can witness your generous gifts in action. Meeting with the actual people you are helping, talking with them about their lives, and seeing the hard work of your charity first-hand is an invaluable experience. At Heifer, we offer study tours for donors, students, and interested people to visit our projects in villages and communities around the world. Imagine supporting a charity that is working on the control and/or cure for diabetes, for example, and having the opportunity to meet someone who was helped by your gift. Think of meeting a cancer survivor who was saved by research that you helped to fund! There's nothing like it in the world.

I've traveled around the world, and I have been privileged to meet with so many recipients of our donors' gifts. I've seen huts transformed into houses, family relationships repaired, and hope returned. What I am struck most by, however, is the amazing ingenuity of recipients.

You see, Heifer International doesn't dictate how

recipients should live their lives. Would you want to be told exactly how to use your talents? With the gift of life-sustaining animals and training, recipients are given the opportunity to map the course of their own lives—sometimes for the first time. They become entrepreneurs, educators, veterinarians, and donors themselves. Fathers and brothers who were forced to leave their families to look for work are able to return to help their loved ones thrive. Children are fed, clothed, and schooled. Disease and violence, often the consequences of hunger and poverty, are eliminated. These changes are happening in communities all around the globe. They are happening because recipients are responsible for creating their own futures.

When I visited China, I had never been outside the United States and had only flown two or three times before. Nothing in my life could have prepared me for what I was about to experience. While I was already moved by the plight of starving families and the work of Heifer International, my experience with the Lee family convinced me that not only could hunger be eradicated, but that peoples' lives could be improved dramatically and permanently.

Before Heifer came to the Lee's, they lived in a one-room home at the base of a mountain. The mountain actually served as the back wall of the house. They owned a half-acre of land where they grew corn, rice, and tea—their only nourishment. Then Heifer came into their lives with dairy goats, and soon the nourishment and small income from the goats began to visibly change their children. They were healthier and stronger. Their skin color improved, and they began to grow. As their lives continued to improve, they began to learn more about running a business and terracing their land—so important in the prevention of land erosion and ensuring their ability to grow crops. The Lee's were always smart people. They just hadn't had the opportunity to build a business.

After three years into the project, the Lee's learned that dairy cattle would be more profitable than goats. Since they had already passed on some of their goats to their neighbors in need, they could sell the remainder to buy a cow, a calf and a bull. They began a successful dairy business. With the income from their dairy business, the Lee's built a new home where their chickens had their own room, the roof was used as a hayloft, and the kitchen featured a tile box with a hole in the middle to build a fire for cooking. This new home may not sound like much to us, but to the Lee's, it was a palace. And this was just the beginning.

The Lee's dairy business became profitable. Their annual income grew from 1,000 Yuan ($125 American at the time) to 300,000 Yuan ($37,500 American). Can you imagine! Every day, after the family was provided for, the Lee's provided milk to more than 100 nearby families.

While I was visiting, one of the Lee boys came out of the house in a tank shirt, worn specifically to show me his muscles. By American standards, he was not a contest winner, but compared to the other boys in the village, this young man had muscles. He wanted me to see what the Heifer project had done for him and his family.

Has charity made a difference in the lives of the Lee's? Of course it has, and since that first trip, I'm no longer surprised to see the miracles performed through donors' gifts every day.

In Uganda, Beatrice and her family had a very hard life. They walked miles twice a day for water from a dirty stream. They cut down bananas from tall trees to sell at the market, competing with hundreds of others selling the same fruit. Beatrice's mother had married at age twelve and had six children. Eventually their father left them, because, as Beatrice told me, he loved them too much to watch them starve to death.

When Beatrice heard that Heifer was coming and her family was going to get a goat, her first response was despair—another mouth to feed, another mess to clean up. But as the milk came, and as Beatrice and her siblings first drank and then began to sell the milk, Beatrice understood that the goat would change their lives forever.

It would nourish her family and provide an income; it would fulfill her dream to go to school.

Since a charity came into Beatrice's life, she has finished school, visited the United States, written a book and was a guest on the Oprah Winfrey show. Beatrice is now an international spokesperson for Heifer and has been featured on *60 Minutes*. I can't wait to see what she will accomplish next! Has charity made a difference in the lives of Beatrice and her family?

Beatrice's story is just one of many. Today, charitable organizations are actively involved in thousands of projects on virtually every continent, making dreams come true for millions of people—donors and recipients alike.

When you begin a circle of giving through the charity of your choice, you will begin to know the people you are helping. You will see your generosity make a huge difference in the world. And your hunger to help others will be fed.

Chapter 2

Donors Come First

Your Charity Should:
Speak directly to your heart
Provide first-hand witness to the fruits of your generosity
Be interested in you: your life, family, desires and goals

There are a multitude of generous donors who give annually to charitable organizations, and we thank them from the bottom of our hearts. But there are also special donors who dedicate themselves to the mission of their charity through multiple, special, or ultimate gifts of their estate. These are donors who are interested in expressing their love and values through their chosen charity. It is the responsibility of charities to fulfill their fiduciary obligations to these individuals. But more importantly, it is their responsibility to build deep relationships with donors who have so generously committed themselves to the organization.

As you begin to look for a charity to use as your vehicle to help bring about a better world, you must look at the organization's mission, its operating procedures, its leadership, and how you as a donor become a vital part.

Here's what I mean. One reason that Heifer Foundation was created was to build an endowment to generate ongoing support for the work of Heifer International. But the other reason the organization was created was for donors. The Foundation was created to give back to donors who selflessly give of their resources to help others. Our mission includes educating donors about charitable planned giving options. We want you to understand the tools that can help you pass on your valuables *and* your values.

I'm reminded of Walter and Jean Aames, and their devoted son, Ted, from Cleveland. Walter and Jean were inspired by the work of Heifer International in the 1950s. They had been blessed with a profitable chicken farm that provided eggs and poultry for them to eat and an income to care for their family's needs. They were loving people, concerned about others, and when they heard about the work of Heifer International, they knew that they had a unique opportunity to give back to a world that had been so generous to them. Farming and farm animals had been very good to them. Why couldn't they do something good with chickens for others? They decided that their family could become personally involved by sending baby chicks to Heifer International to help others who were less fortunate begin a promising future.

As the years passed, the Aames' continued their support of Heifer International in a variety of ways, and when I met them, they were lovely seniors who were interested in creating a plan that would reflect their family values for generations to come.

I traveled to Cleveland on a beautiful fall morning. The trees created an explosion of color, every shade of red, orange, and yellow. I left the airport with my map and drove from interstate highway to country roads, to country routes, to dirt farm roads, and finally to a one-way dirt road over a covered bridge. I was there. I finally arrived at the home of Jean and Walter Aames who stood watching as I pulled into their front yard—there was no driveway.

Their home was a beautiful white two-story farmhouse with lace curtains and wooden rocking chairs on the front porch. I could hear them laughing as I turned to lock my car doors. Walter said, "Janet, no one will take anything way out here, except the raccoons!" From that point on, I was the "city girl."

We spent the day together, touring the farm and becoming fast friends. Walter led me down dirt paths and across fields of beautiful Murray Gray cattle and grass so tall it reached my fingertips as we walked. Walter shared stories about his childhood with me and how special this farm was to him. We walked the fields for almost an hour sharing the special times in Walter and Jean's lives and talking about how much Heifer had meant to them both.

As Walter continued the tour through the barn and chicken houses, I was struck by how much this family had given to others, and I was inspired by their desire to continue to give. "Walter," I said, "your gifts to Heifer have changed the lives of people all over the world. Your chickens have helped your neighbors in Asia, Africa, Eastern Europe, Latin America and even here in our own United States." Walter seemed pleased with my words, even though he stood silent and worked with the ancient equipment he was demonstrating.

Unlike the chicken house, the aroma of the house was delightful when we returned. Jean had been cooking all afternoon, preparing a meal for us from the food she picked from her own garden or the products they produced on the farm. You haven't lived until you've tasted stuffed zucchini and a homemade double-layer chocolate cake from Jean's kitchen!

As Jean brought out the cake, their son Ted came into the house. He shared his thoughts and feelings about the coming years on the farm. He told me of his desire for the farm to continue to produce income for the family and eventually go to charity to help change a world in great need. Walter and Jean agreed with their son. Walter explained that their estate had been set up so that after his and Jean's lifetime, a portion of the farm would go to Heifer to continue its work. What a great day for Walter, Jean, Ted and their charity of choice. Their desires to help family and friends around the world would be fulfilled.

When you choose your charity, choose one that will take the time to get to know you, meet your family, and truly care about your life. Charities that will build a meaningful relationship with you will honor you and your desires.

About three weeks after visiting Jean and Walter, I received a call in the early morning. It was Jean. She called to tell me that Walter had passed away that night. She wanted me to know that the past three weeks had been the best in a long time for Walter. He had been reminded that he made a difference in the world through his charity. He had helped to create a better place to live. He also found peace because he had put his desires in writing, and he trusted me to carry them out. The leadership of your chosen charity has more responsibility than just to their organization. The leadership must do everything possible to carry out your wishes. Receiving that call from Jean reinforced my commitment to listening, spending time with donors, and having a true interest in their daily lives.

Did You Know?

Charitable giving instruments, such as trusts, annuities, and endowments can provide financial security to donors through ongoing income and tax deductions. Helping yourself first ensures you can help others.

Donors have to come first. A variety of charitable instruments exist to help donors meet their own financial needs so that giving to others does not create a hardship for themselves or their families. Every donor is different. Your families, goals, and dreams are different. Your properties and possessions are different. Your commitments to other charities are different. So why shouldn't your plans be different too?

The most important role of your charity is to know and understand you, to carry out your wishes. They need to work closely with you and your advisors to ensure your financial security so that you can fulfill your philanthropic goals *and* family obligations.

YOUR CHARITY AS PART OF YOUR TEAM

While my role is in dealing directly with the charitable portion of your plan, you should always consult other financial and legal advisors - those who view your entire estate plan, to help you make the right decisions as you seek to meet your financial, family, and charitable desires. Like any team, all of us bring valuable, yet different, expertise to your process. And all of us need to understand your value system and work with open minds to meet your goals and desires. You are the person we need to please.

Trusted team members typically include:

» Certified Public Accountant (CPA)

» Attorney

» Chartered Life Underwriter (CLU) or Certified Financial Planner (CFP)

» Trust Officer or Broker

» Charitable Representative

CERTIFIED PUBLIC ACCOUNTANT

Most people have reasonably frequent contact with a Certified Public Accountant (CPA). Although the CPA completes your annual income tax return, he or she can also give you valuable advice when you are making a major decision. The CPA who is open to discussing planning opportunities can explain various options and provide suggestions and recommendations about the benefits of those plans. I have worked with many CPAs who understand and share donors' values—professionals who are able to consider and present the hard numbers within the context of their client's desires.

ATTORNEY

Attorneys are necessarily involved in the creation of wills and trusts. Your attorney has a professional responsibility to evaluate plans and major property transfers and will advise you about the legal methods or ways that transfers can be done and how they will impact your overall plan. If you have a large estate, it is especially important to work with an attorney who specializes in tax and estate planning. Congress has dramatically changed the field of taxation during the past decade so you will want to be sure your attorney specializes in taxation and estate planning.

CHARTERED LIFE UNDERWRITER OR CERTIFIED FINANCIAL PLANNER

Since life insurance is found in nearly all estates and is now being used to provide estate tax liquidity in larger estates, you need very good counsel to purchase good quality plans. Life insurance plans have increased appreciably in quality and overall benefit to the consumer as a result of tremendous competition in the field. However, you want to make sure that you are buying your insurance from a highly rated company. Life insurance companies are rated through A.M. Best Company, Moody's Investors Service, Standard & Poors Corporation, and Duff & Phelps rating companies. Working with a qualified CLU or CFP will enable you to make certain that you have a very good plan that is properly secured by safe investments.

TRUST OFFICER OR BROKER

Many of our donors and friends listen to a trust officer or a broker who has helped them with their investments. Trust officers and brokers know the total estate picture and can counsel you on how your investment plans now can ensure your estate will "carry you through". With the advice of your broker or trust officer you can continue to invest well. There are always good investments that provide a fair return with good safety. You simply need to know enough about investing to see that you are taking advantage of those good investments. Furthermore, you should attempt to conserve the estate from the ravages of taxation. Using the appropriate methods, you can save income tax, reduce your estate tax or even bypass capital gain on the sale of an appreciated asset. Your trust officer or broker should know these methods or consult a charitable representative. These methods of conservation are essential if you are to get maximum benefit from your property. The advice of an officer or broker can be invaluable as you are accumulating your estate.

All of these advisors perform a very key role in keeping your family's financial ship afloat and oriented toward the objectives that you set.

YOUR CHARITABLE REPRESENTATIVE

You have chosen your charity to be the tool you use to make a lasting difference in the world. When Jean and Walter Aames selected Heifer Foundation to carry out their charitable wishes, they believed in the cause of Heifer. More than that, they believed that Heifer Foundation was trustworthy, qualified, knowledgeable and of the same heart and mind as themselves. They believed that the Foundation would remain committed—legally and personally—to understanding and fulfilling their desires in life and after death.

As you examine charitable organizations, consider the following:

» The qualifications of the staff
» The roles and responsibilities as your fiduciary
» The role of trustee
» The operational excellence of the organization
» The variety and flexibility of charitable giving instruments and programs
» The availability of leadership and educational information/programs

QUALIFIED STAFF

Charitable organizations are typically staffed with individuals experienced in the areas of non-profit management, planned charitable giving, finance, administration, and trusteeship to carry out donors' desires. The Board of Trustees ensures that accountability, stewardship and fiduciary responsibilities are above reproach. Donors also need to know who will be responsible for investing their funds. For example, Heifer foundation works with leading partner consultants and premiere global firms to ensure the growth and stability of our donors' trusts and endowments. Because we don't personally invest your money, we spend the time and resources necessary to get to know you and your family personally, to better understand and carry out your express wishes. We do this by carefully managing our consultants and taking responsibility for your assets, trusts, etc.

ROLES AND RESPONSIBILITIES AS YOUR FIDUCIARY

Charitable organizations will serve as your fiduciary, which means that they are legally bound to carry out your wishes and act in the best interests of you and your beneficiaries for the exclusive purpose of providing benefits and defraying reasonable administrative expenses. We must use care, skill, prudence and diligence to be sure that your gifts are administered according to your wishes, designations, and documents; and we must take responsibility for your assets (stocks, bonds, certificates of deposit, etc.) within the jurisdiction of courts and government agencies.

Another important responsibility of a fiduciary deals with the diversification of investments. Like a financial management company, charities will usually distribute investments among several managers with various investment styles consistent with governing investment guidelines. Charities are responsible, as your fiduciary, to prudently select investment management options and ensure that those investment options remain appropriate. That's why our due diligence is so extensive. It is important to know if your charity objectively selects investment consultants, managers, or firms and conducts frequent and in-depth evaluation processes. Most charities have qualified staff to analyze financial information, performance data, portfolio breakdowns, investment objectives, and industry ratings.

The Role of Trustee

Simply put, the role of the trustee is to manage the business of your trusts, annuities, or endowments. Someone must be identified to prepare and file IRS forms, distribute funds to beneficiaries (including other charities), and review and process paperwork as appropriate. The trustee can be you, a family member, your bank, an attorney, or your charity. Often donors don't want to place the burden of such a responsibility on their family members.

The leaders of charitable organizations can also serve as your trustee. With a diligent and qualified staff, all of the paperwork and checks and balances required to fulfill your plan are carefully managed and filed through your charity. Heifer Foundation serves as the trustee for many of our donors. In fact, we will serve as a trustee without charge if your plan allocates 50% or more of your estate to the Foundation.

OPERATIONAL EXCELLENCE

If you want your donation to achieve the greatest impact on a world in need, it makes sense that you should care deeply about how your charity of choice runs its business. The National Committee on Planned Giving, the Association of Fundraising Professionals, and the American Council of Gift Annuities recommends strict standards to ensure donors' bill of rights. These rights are:

I.   To be informed of the organization's mission, of the way the organization intends to use donated resources, and of its capacity to use donations effectively for their intended purposes.

II. To be informed of the identity of those serving on the organization's governing board, and to expect the board to exercise prudent judgment in its stewardship responsibilities.

III. To have access to the organization's most recent
    financial statements.

IV. To be assured their gifts will be used for the
    purposes for which they were given.

 V. To receive appropriate acknowledgment and
    recognition.

VI. To be assured that information about their
    donation is handled with respect and with
    confidentiality to the extent provided by law.

VII. To expect that all relationships with individuals
    representing organizations of interest to the
    donor will be professional in nature.

VIII. To be informed whether those seeking donations
    are volunteers, employees of the organization or
    hired solicitors.

IX. To have the opportunity for their names to be
    deleted from mailing lists that an organization
    may intend to share.

 X. To feel free to ask questions when making a
    donation and to receive prompt, truthful and
    forthright answers."

For organizations like Heifer Foundation, whose
primary purpose is to provide support for another
entity (in our case, Heifer International), the most
reasonable measurement of efficient spending is either

the ratio of total expense to total assets or total expense to total net assets. To meet an excellent rating, we strive to maintain our total expenses within a 3% to 7% range of total assets managed on an annual basis. In addition, to level the effects of stock market volatility and large donations, organizations like Heifer Foundation average total assets over a three-year period. Of course, all charitable organizations' financial reports are considered public information and are available to donors and potential donors.

CHARITABLE GIVING INSTRUMENTS AND PROGRAMS

Perhaps you are like our friend Mr. Angelo who wants to use his stock to continue the work of his charity while receiving a stable quarterly income. Charitable organizations have been issuing gift annuities for many years. It is a wonderful way to help fund college educations, supplement a retirement plan or help children provide added financial support for aging parents.

Maybe you're more like Lester and Mary Ford who established the Ford Family Endowment through Heifer Foundation to be sure their family values would be passed on from generation to generation. While Lester and Mary began the endowment together, it will continue to grow after they are both gone, ensuring that all members of their growing family will know the importance of sharing wealth with others.

Whether a trust, annuity or endowment is best for your goals, your charitable organization must educate you about their planned charitable giving instruments and then carry out your plan according to your desires. Chapters 3 through 7 are devoted to explaining charitable planned giving instruments.

AVAILABILITY TO SERVE DONORS

The number one priority of the leadership of your chosen charity should be you. On an average, I spend 60% of my time one-on-one with our wonderful donors. The most important use of that time is to build a truly meaningful relationship. How can I serve as your fiduciary or trustee if I don't know you? How can you entrust the future of your values to me if you don't know me? Like a doctor, I am privy to your most private information. But unlike a doctor, we become partners in accomplishing your dreams.

I have experienced such joy by the relationships that have been created through my work over the years. I have been present at donors' weddings, birthdays, anniversary parties, church programs, dinners, and many other special events. I have built friendships with remarkably wise and kind people whom I love. But, as with all relationships, heartbreaks come, too. I have attended more funeral and memorial services than I care to remember. I have been present when individuals have moved from their lifelong home or sold property that has been in their families for generations. I have seen the heartbreaking faces of children who have relocated their parents to a nursing facility or hospice for their final days. With each event, good or bad, comes a better understanding of our donors and an opportunity to provide genuine support as I seek to help them fulfill their desires. You come first.

Planned Giving Instruments: Helping You Help Others

Introduction

What kind of world do you want your grandchildren and their children to inherit? How can you ensure your valuables and your values will be passed on? In the foreword of this book, I wrote about a woman very dear to me who slowly sold her farm to support herself as she aged. After capital gains taxes were paid and the last plot of farmland was gone, she spent her final years in a nursing facility, her care subsidized by her family and the government. All her life she was devoted to helping children—first her own five, and then the school children of Arkansas. It was her dream to provide something to children all over the world one day. But in the end, she didn't have enough to even care for herself. It didn't have to end that way.

I've run the calculations many times, and they are heartbreaking. With the right plan, this woman could have accomplished all of her wishes. She could have lived her life out in her home, left an inheritance for her children, and provided a generous gift to her charity. Through a Charitable Remainder Trust, she could have given her property to charity, and the charity in turn would have given her the appraised value for funding the trust. Her 2,000-acre farm would have provided approximately $140,000 annual income to her for life and then to her five children. With good investments by the charity, her $2 million estate would have turned into approximately $5.5 million over the lifetime of her heirs, and the charity would have eventually received approximately $3.5 million. With the right plan, her estate would have taken excellent care of her until her death and dramatically improved the lives of many, many children.

Certainly not everyone is just a step away from losing everything. But all of us *are* concerned about maximizing our estates for longevity, ensuring our valuables reach their destination without being consumed by taxes and creating a legacy that matches how we live our lives. Some of us are just starting to consider who gets what, when, and how, while still others of us see retirement far in the future. None of us relish the thought of planning for the end of our lives, but creating a plan is the most loving thing you can do for yourself and your loved ones.

The following chapters are designed to provide greater insight into the variety of charitable planned giving instruments available to help you achieve your personal and charitable objectives in the most tax-wise and advantageous manner possible. Whether you want to create a legacy that you can watch grow while you are still young or ensure your spouse is supported after your death, each planned giving instrument is designed to deliver unique benefits—in life and after death.

As you'll learn from the many beloved donors whose plans and processes are discussed, there *is* a way to take care of yourself so that you can take better care of your family—and a world in great need. There *is* a way to accomplish your unique and heartfelt desires to begin an unending circle of giving.

Chapter 3

Your Life. Your Goals. Your Plan.

I received this letter from a young man named Frank one warm summer morning.

Dear Janet,

Thank you for your wonderful card and letter telling me how much the Heifer Family cares for me. I appreciate your continued prayers and support.

I have found out that anybody can become a widower. There aren't any special qualifications. It happens in less time than it takes to draw a breath. It doesn't require the planning, for example that it takes to become a husband or a father or any of the other ritual roles of manhood. And it is neither dramatic nor majestic—really more a snapshot than a feature film. For such a monumental thing to be accomplished in seconds defies logic—in fact, it's almost insulting. But there it is."

My wife, Natalie died of cancer on a sunny June morning, when the grip of a Wisconsin winter had finally relaxed. It was the last day of school, and I'd assured my two middle sons, then in first and third grades that nothing could happen to Mommy in the one hour it would take to pick up their report cards. Our teenager was getting ready for her senior prom; the littlest, just turned four, was downstairs with Michelle, our caregiver. I was looking forward to an hour's sleep.

All night, I'd napped on the floor near our bed. Between Natalie's low moans and the thump-hiss of the oxygen tank, we'd managed little rest. So, newly showered, I lay down beside my wife of twenty years, my best friend for most of my life.

I don't believe in signs, but I've come to think that the atmosphere in a room does take on the coloration of a significant change. For some reason, I leaned close to Natalie's ear as she breathed in, and then, thirty seconds later, slowly out, and I whispered, "It's been my privilege to be married to you." Natalie gave a kind of hiccup, and then she was gone. She had just turned 40 and I was 45.

It is of extreme importance to me to prepare a will that will take care of my four children and the matters of this world that have become so urgent to me. Can you help?

Sincerely, Frank

I can't express to you the importance of finding a charity that has a vision and dream of putting you first. A charity that has a vision for the future that will include those who have gone before us, you, your family, and those who will come after us. What an honor and privilege it is to serve individuals who care so much.

On average, we Americans are living longer and longer. According to the U.S. Census Bureau in 2004, "life expectancy in the United States increased from 51 to 80 for females and from 48 to 74 for males over the last century. The projection for the year 2050 is 87 years for females and 81 years for men. Some analysts believe that life expectancy in the United States and other rich nations is approaching a biological limit, but no slowdown is apparent yet."

These numbers are just averages. How many people do you know who are well into their 80s? At Heifer, we had a lovely 111 year-old donor, and many more who are fast approaching that age. The truth is we don't know how long we're going to be on earth. Some lives are cut way too short. Others extend well into old age. Either way, we need a plan to ensure income for the rest of our lives, to provide for our families, and to help our brothers and sisters in need.

It is my desire—through this book and through my work at Heifer Foundation—to give back to our wonderful donors and friends a way to help themselves so that they can continue to create lasting circles of giving.

You have a goal for your life. You are here on earth to pass on your values as well as your valuables. You have worked extremely hard to earn what you have, and you've saved for the coming years. One's lifespan is unpredictable, which is why you need a financial plan to be ensured of income for the rest of your life, and to be confident that your desire to continue to make a difference in the world will be fulfilled.

It is essential that you have a plan so that your desires will be carried out. I can't overstate this. You've given of your life and resources so that others may be helped, but you can't help others unless you put yourself first. Your charity must put you first: by getting to know you and your family, your dreams and your values. Only then can they help you accomplish your desire to bring about change in the world.

RETIREMENT

At Heifer Foundation, our donor who passed away when she was 111 created an estate plan with her advisors to provide for her medical, living expenses and even death expenses—with plenty of discretionary income included —

without the assistance from family or government programs no matter how long she lived. Most important, her plan was created to preserve her independence and dignity.

You must create a plan that is designed to conserve the assets you worked so hard to earn, no matter how long you live. Before you consider helping others, you must think about your own retirement, your independence, and your financial stability.

DISTRIBUTION OF PROPERTY

We are born into families and then we create our families of choice—those with whom we share a deep connection. Who gets the home? How many insurance policies do you own? What do you want to happen to your stocks and bonds? Most people are surprised by how much they own when they begin to list their assets. You have significant relationships and a goal of what you want to give after you're gone.

There are many people to think about when planning the distribution of your property. For you, your family of choice may consist of the college you attended or the friends you've had for 50 years. What about the hospital that took such good care of your spouse of 55 years who suffered so terribly with cancer? How could you forget your church or synagogue that supported you through some very difficult times? Your plan must include the benefits for your family of choice and for others:

» Family of Choice

» College or University

» Place of Worship

» Service or Charitable Organization

» Hospital

» Friends

VALUE TRANSFER

There are keys to what we call value transfer. You transfer your values through example. By the way you live your life and care for your family and others in need. To transfer your values it takes:

» Planning

» Good advisors who talk to you about your entire life, not just profits & losses

» Estate conservation, because you never know how long you will be on earth

» Benefits for your family of choice

» Benefits for others

If you don't decide through planning what you want to happen after you're gone, the government will decide. You have two choices: you or the government. As much as I love my country, I don't want the government determining where my funds will go. So I have an estate plan, and I know on my dying day where my funds will go.

They will go to my children, and eventually they will go to help a world in need.

Your charity should help you first, so you can help others. Your charity must create an atmosphere of trust until death—and beyond—and this can only be accomplished by stewardship, accountability, relationships, and a total commitment to putting you and your desires first. Charities must specialize in helping people achieve their charitable objectives in the most tax-wise and advantageous manner possible. There are several goals you need to accomplish. They include lifetime income, tax benefits, and estate planning so that all you have worked so hard for during your life will go to family and the charities you love. Charities can be of assistance in all of these areas, but they must absolutely be committed to carrying out your goals and desires after the gift matures.

The legacy that is created with your gift will continue your caring values after your lifetime, generating perpetual support to help others. Your legacy passes on much more than your valuables. It is an extension of your principles of living and speaks volumes about your life.

Chapter 4

Trusts

"Put not your trust in money. Put your money into trust."
Benjamin Franklin

A Winning Combination

With a charitable remainder trust, you and/or a loved one receive a lifetime income from your donated assets. The remainder goes to a world in need. It's a win/win scenario for generous donors.

FROM SADNESS TO JOY

Paul and George Wright are brothers. They look alike and sound alike. They are both kind and generous, small framed, smart, but unassuming. The Wright brothers have lived their whole lives on the farm that was given to them by their father who started out with one cow. He began to grow rice and over time developed a beautiful, productive rice farm. As the Wright brothers grew older, they joined their father in the fields, and when their father died, the farm became a joint venture for the two of them. This was their life. They married, lived across a road from each other, and together raised George and his wife Judith's children together.

When Paul called my office, he and his brother were in their early seventies. "I think maybe it's time to go out of the farming business," he said. "Could you use some old equipment?" It was a cold winter morning when he called. I could imagine the wind whipping across their fields and was reminded of the hard life of farming. Big business may have invented the term 24/7 a few years back to talk about their unwavering commitments, but farmers have been living 24/7 since the beginning of agriculture. It takes a certain kind of love, devotion, and stamina to make a farm work. I knew the lives of the Wright brothers were about to change dramatically.

I have a special love for farmers. I didn't grow up on a farm myself, but you can't live in Arkansas without knowing farmers. I think working with the land and caring for animals gives farmers certain clarity about the world —a wisdom about their own power and limitations—that can get lost on those of us in busy offices. I couldn't wait to visit with the Wrights.

Have you ever stood next to a combine? I would never be accused of being a tall woman, but then again, no one's tall next to a combine. What fun I had that day. We toured the farm, and Paul and George shared the purpose and story behind every piece of equipment, some dating back to when the two of them were boys.

After a lovely day of walking across fields and in and out of barns, we sat down at Paul's table to talk about their phone call. Both of the brothers felt strongly about making a difference in the world. They were raised as compassionate men and wanted to continue their family legacy. At their age, they could no longer run the farm, and their children had created successful careers of their own elsewhere. They were committed to helping hungry families around the world, but they also shared that George's spouse was ill and required considerable medical support. They were both concerned about being able to take care of themselves and their spouses for the years to come without the income from their farm. It was obvious that giving the gift of their equipment was indeed a difficult and important decision, and one that would change their lives forever. But I assured them that Heifer could help.

After discussing a variety of options, we decided to create a Charitable Remainder Unitrust for each of the brothers from the value of the farm equipment. The trust in turn would provide tax benefits and ensure an annual income for the lifetimes of both families. The remainder would go to Heifer Foundation to help eradicate hunger and poverty and continue the Wright family's legacy of caring for others.

After an appraiser valued the equipment, the trust was set up, and a date was set to auction off the equipment on the Wright's farm. This, I knew, would be the hardest day. Saying goodbye to what the brothers had known their whole lives would be emotional. The equipment held memories of their father and mother, their childhoods, business success, marriages, and their own children. But an extraordinary thing happens when you give a gift.

The day of the auction was beautiful, crisp and sunny, full of the sounds of the outdoors—chirping crickets and tree tops rustling. All of the equipment had been washed and lined up in the sun. The small hand tools were placed on tables with festive decorations. The best barbeque I've had in a long time was served up on colorful paper plates. It looked and felt like a fairground! As the trucks began to turn into the farm, I shared with Paul and George how wonderful this day would be for their family and their charity. Their beloved gift would truly make a difference to so many around the world, just as they had hoped. And it has.

Everyone who came that day went home with several special gifts – one of farm equipment; one of helping a neighbor; and one of helping a world in need. That day the Wright brothers shared their values and generosity with the farmers who came from miles. As every hoe, hose, and combine was auctioned off to feed hungry people, Paul and George felt true joy in their decision. They also felt secure about the future of their families. It was obvious in their smiles and hugs.

Paul liked the way the Charitable Remainder Unitrust worked for him and his wife Linda. Because they have a close family but no children of their own, they established a trust for each of their nine nieces and nephews, now in their 50's and 60's. After they receive a lifetime income, the remainder will go into the Paul and Linda Wright Endowment to help other children around the world in perpetuity.

HOME IS WHERE THE HEART IS

William and Theda Avery can tell you that a charity's commitment beyond your property is so important. The Averys owned a beautiful home in Seattle, Washington. If you've ever been to Seattle you know its renowned natural beauty is no exaggeration. The Avery's dark wood house was nestled in a grove of cedar and pine trees. It was truly a retreat in the midst of nature. They loved their home. They loved the way the light crept in through the tree limbs in the morning and the way they felt a million miles from civilization at night when the only thing they could see when looking out the windows was their own reflection. For many, many years its rustic beauty was the backdrop to full, love-filled lives.

A time came, however, when William and Theda knew they should consider moving into a retirement center. They called me to see how they could receive lifetime income and still help a world in need. It was their desire to give their beautiful home to charity so that it could be a blessing to others as it had been to them. While this seemed to make the idea of the move easier, it was certainly no small decision.

For several months, we worked with William and Theda to make sure that all of their desires were being met, both financial and charitable. As we went through the process of setting up the charitable remainder trust with their financial advisor, there were days of joy as we discussed all of those who would be helped because of this wonderful gift. But there were days of great sadness as memories were shared. The anxiousness brought about by change, the anticipation of a different lifestyle and the feeling of loss all surfaced during the coming days.

The day the deed was signed over to the charity was actually a day of relief for the Averys. Theda shared, "I know now that this is the right thing for all of us. This house will help create another home for the couple that is purchasing it, it will secure our future in the new retirement center, and it will help people in a far-away country make a home for their children." Theda was talking about a circle of giving. She and her husband were fed from feeding others. And we were fed by committing ourselves to their needs, their decisions, and their process. What a great day as we partnered with William and Theda. They are both still very active volunteers for Heifer, and we cherish them.

THE FUTURE IS NOW

Sam and Stella Marie Vincent's story began on a 1983 vacation. The family went horseback riding one morning and rode a rubber raft on a swift river in the afternoon. At the end of the day, Sam thought about how he had never done either before, and it was fun to try something new. Sparked by this thought, he made a list of other things that he wanted to do someday and shared the list with his family. A few months later, his wife saw that a nearby nonprofit tourist railroad was giving a free class on railroading. One item on her husband's list was "operate a locomotive" so he went, and he got hooked. After many more classes, he became a qualified locomotive engineer, and now a couple of times a month, he and his wife put on their red bandanas and bib overalls and play trains.

As you can see, my friends Stella Marie and Sam Vincent have very full lives, packed with adventures and plenty of time for volunteering. They are also active in their church, and they diligently practice home energy conservation. These wonderful people care deeply about our world. They say that their quest to reduce energy consumption has taught them the importance of investing today for future dividends. As Sam says, "This mindset has given me a special fondness for planning ahead."

Another item on Sam's list of things he wants to do is to make a greater contribution to the world. After thinking long and hard about where they'd like their estate to go at the end of their lives, the Vincents decided that it should first provide additional income to their children and then go to several favorite charities. They felt good about showing their children how much they are loved *and* how important it is to share with those in need. But then they both had a nagging feeling. Who, exactly, would be overseeing their donations after they've gone? How effectively would their donations be used? Ultimately, their idea didn't bring them peace of mind. So, they decided to investigate alternatives.

When I met with the Vincents, we talked about their desire to watch their donations change the world. After discussing their options, they decided to start their giving plan sooner, during their lives for several good reasons:

» Giving while you're still living causes you to become clear about the objectives of your gifts. While this takes considerable thought, it's much better than leaving the future up to estate executives or lawyers.

» While giving away what you've spent a lifetime to build is a difficult concept to embrace, as the money is given away, a different, more freeing attitude about financial management develops.

» Charitable giving while living offers you a chance to gain feedback about how your donation will be used. It gives you reason to either confirm or change your giving plans as you acquire more information.

With all of this in mind, Sam and Stella Marie Vincent set up a Charitable Remainder Unitrust. Not only will their accumulated assets pass on to their specified charities after death, establishing a Unitrust helped them in several other ways:

» Tax payments on large capital gains on stocks were avoided;

» Tax deductions were gained; and

» A lifetime income stream that will grow as the assets appreciate was ensured.

Now, Sam and Stella Marie feel confident about their involvement with their charities. They transferred some securities into an account that is managed by Heifer Foundation, which meets their desires for both Heifer and another favorite charity, which are listed as equal beneficiaries. The accumulated assets will pass on to the charities the Vincents trust to carry out their desires after their lifetime. As Sam says, "We feel this winning combination has put our personal train on the right track."

THE GIFT OF LOVE

It's hard to find the words to describe the bond between parents and children. Blessed. Rich. Expansive. Nothing quite covers it. The love is indescribable. We love our children so deeply that most of us wouldn't hesitate for a split second to agree to do anything to save their lives. But parenting rarely comes down to such heroics. We teach by example day in and day out, hoping and praying that our children will grow into compassionate, responsible adults.

The Fairchilds are no different. Just like us, they love their four children (three daughters and one son) indescribably. The children are now in their 50s—an accomplished major airline pilot, a lawyer, and two doctors. And yes, they are compassionate and responsible, traits they learned from their parents.

The Fairchilds moved in their later years to a retirement village in Colorado to be near their daughter who helps with their needs. Christmas time is always the best because of the wonderful snowfall, and the skiing is a treat for their five grandchildren from Miami. Like most busy families, the Fairchilds struggle to get their entire family together, and on the occasional holiday when they are all present, the dining room table is now fully opened to accommodate the growing family.

In planning their estate, the Fairchilds wanted to show their children how much they love them, but they also wanted to illustrate the value of helping to save the world. They're blessed in many, many ways and recognize that not everyone is. The Fairchilds themselves aren't in need of extra income, and they believe that their children have created wonderful lives for themselves. How could they show their children how much they are loved while also fulfilling their own personal desire to significantly help those less fortunate?

I admire the Fairchilds. My husband and I, like so many parents, worked hard to raise our children to make good choices and show compassion to others. Most of us as parents share the experience of wanting to give everything to our children, but we know that *not* doing so is often a greater gift, a gift of love.

After meeting with Mr. and Mrs. Fairchild and discussing their desires, we created the perfect option. With the gift of one of their properties, the Fairchilds set up a Charitable Remainder Unitrust - Term Only that provides an annual income to each child for ten years. After that, the remainder goes to Heifer Foundation and another beloved charity. All of the Fairchilds desires have been met. Their gifts and values have been passed on to their children and their charity of choice. Another win/win.

THE GOLDEN YEARS

Many of you are in your 40s and 50s and have been successful in your careers. You've been blessed. You make a decent living, maybe a little better than some others, and you're starting to look toward retirement. Not only would you like to retire comfortably, you'd like to make a difference in the world. Perhaps you've always given to charity. Now you'd like to create a legacy that says how important it is to weigh in on world issues.

Planned giving is not just for people who are already in their golden years. If you were to donate a gift of $200,000 while you were in your 30s, for example— perhaps an inheritance of property —you could create a Charitable Remainder Retirement Trust and receive an income of more than $85,000 annually once you retire. Your charity, the remainder beneficiary, receives more than $1 million from the wise investment of your original $200,000 gift.

THE BASICS ABOUT CHARITABLE REMAINDER TRUSTS

For many years trusts have grown in popularity. And it's no wonder. Considered one of the most flexible

Benefits of Trusts

~ *You bypass capital gains taxes on the capital gain assets placed in trust*

~ *You decide what percentage of the trust you want to receive as annual income*

~*You designate the trustee*

~ *The remainder of your trust becomes your legacy for building a better world*

instruments, trusts meet a variety of financial and philanthropic goals. They provide income for you and your family, deliver tax benefits and typically increase the value of your original philanthropic gift. Simply put, a trust is a way for charitably-minded individuals to make gifts, while preserving economic security for themselves and their loved ones.

The fundamental charitable trust arrangement involves a transfer of property to a trustee selected by you with the promise that it will be held according to your instructions and for a specific period of time. From the simplest to the most complex, every trust is based upon this principle and contains the same basic elements.

A living trust is one that you create while you are alive and meets your needs for management services and for family and charitable beneficiaries following death. A testamentary trust is created upon death by instructions contained in your will.

How Trusts Work

A Charitable Remainder Unitrust is set up to pay a fixed percentage of principal to one or more income beneficiaries annually (based on market performance). The annual payment must be paid for the life of the income beneficiary, or for a term not to exceed 20 years. The trust can be set up to provide for annual payments equally to the beneficiaries, and then to a survivor, until the survivor's death. Payments must be made at least annually, although they can be made more frequently if desired.

Trust Options

Charitable Remainder Unitrust. As the donor, you place property, stock, cash and/or other assets in a trust and specify that payments from the trust be made to you and/or one or more other persons for life. After the death of the beneficiary, the remainder of the trust goes to charity.

Charitable Remainder Unitrust Term Only. You may choose to have the payment made from a trust for a set period of time, up to 20 years. The Fairchilds chose this kind of trust so that an income could be provided to their children for the term of ten years, at which point the remainder of the trust went to Heifer Foundation to end hunger and poverty. The Fairchilds were able to provide for their children and save estate and capital gains taxes on the property while fulfilling their desire to help others in need.

Charitable Remainder Unitrust Plus Term. This is a Charitable Remainder Unitrust for one or two lives and then an additional term of years (up to 20) for other individuals before going to the charity. For example, you may want your trust to provide a lifetime income for you and your spouse. After you both die, your children—or other designated beneficiaries—receive an annual income for up to 20 years before the remainder goes to your charity.

Charitable Remainder Retirement Unitrust. This giving instrument enables donors to invest in their futures as well as their charities. Similar to standard retirement accounts, your charity invests your donation in the market for growth. Once you retire, your trust should have grown over the years, and you receive an annual income for life. Upon death, the remainder of your trust goes to fulfill your charitable desires.

Charitable Remainder Lead Unitrust. In a certain sense, this is the opposite of a Charitable Remainder Unitrust. Whereas the Charitable Remainder Trust pays income to you for a period of time and then pays the remainder to your charity, the Lead Trust pays income to your charity for a period of time and then pays the remainder to you or other designated individuals.

Charitable Remainder Flip Unitrust. This trust is funded by property and works like a Net Income Only Unitrust (which pays the beneficiary the lesser of the trust's amount or the trust's actual net income) until the property is sold and then it flips to a standard Charitable Remainder Unitrust. This provides a good benefit to donors since they will be able to receive a greater benefit from the Standard Charitable Remainder Unitrust.

FUNDING TRUSTS

Working with your estate planning advisors can help you choose the best way to fund your gifts for maximum tax and estate management advantages. The assets you may choose include:
» Cash and Personal Property
» Stocks and Bonds
» Livestock
» Real Estate
» Family Business
» Retirement Plans and Life Insurance

Whether securities or real estate, if you've owned the asset for more than a year and the value is higher than your cost, you may want to consider placing the property in a charitable trust.

The trustee of a charitable trust can sell appreciated assets without incurring tax on the capital gain. Then the entire proceeds, less closing costs, are invested to provide a flow of income to you and/or your family as income beneficiary(ies) of the trust. At the end of the trust, normally upon the death of the income recipient(s), whatever is left will then be distributed to the charity(ies) you name in the trust.

Were you to sell your property yourself, a significant amount of the sale proceeds could be lost to taxes. But with a Charitable Remainder Trust, the full proceeds are invested to meet the goals of the trust. Think of the extra income this could mean to you during your lifetime. The beautiful thing is that you can make a deferred gift to your charity and still provide income for yourself and your family of choice. You also get an immediate income tax deduction, avoid capital gains tax, and possibly save estate tax.

TRUST INVESTMENTS

Trusts are invested for each individual's needs in terms of income requirements and personal desires. For example, if you require a dependable income impervious to market shifts, it would be prudent to invest your trust funds in a larger percentage of fixed income bonds. If you require less dependability and are open to more flexibility, a greater portion of your trust may be invested in equity funds. Either way, your charity should practice diversification and allocation and adhere to strict codes of ethics. Heifer Foundation, for example, works with premier partner consultants and investment firms to ensure the growth and stability of our donors' trusts. Additionally, we will not invest in firearms, tobacco, gambling, alcohol, and environmental degradation.

CHOOSING YOUR TRUSTEE

Your trustee is the person responsible for the overall management of your trust. Management includes maintaining all of the paperwork, handling the tax work, distributing funds, and keeping additional records required by the IRS. If you are not interested in serving as your own trustee, you could choose from the following options:
» Bank
» Charity
» Attorney
» Family Member

Many charities can serve as your trustee. Look for a qualified staff with years of experience in this role. At Heifer, we are the trustee of many donors' trusts, and we provide this service at no cost to those who have named us at least a 50% beneficiary of the trust.

What You Can Use to Fund Your Gifts
~ *Cash and Personal Property*
~ *Stocks and Bonds*
~ *Livestock*
~ *Real Estate*
~ *Family Business*
~ *Retirement Plans and Life Insurance*

CALCULATING THE BENEFITS OF YOUR TRUST

The following are just a few examples of the income benefits of Charitable Remainder Trusts.

The data required to calculate your trust includes:

» Your Age

» Market value of the property you're considering as your gift

» Estimated cost of the property when bought

» Your tax bracket

» What you want to receive as income from the trust

Charitable Remainder Unitrust

John Jones, 65; Mary Jones, 60

Trust Principal:	$200,000
Bypass of gains saves:	$32,000
Charitable deduction received at age 65:	$51,470
Annual income received based on 6.52% rate:	$12,000
Charity receives:	$321,687

The percentage you choose for your return must be a minimum of 5%, but can be more depending on what you and the trustee agree to. Most people choose a lower rate to provide more growth in the trust and thus more protection against inflation. If you desire a higher percentage, you risk dipping into principle, which could affect your income in future years.

Charitable Remainder Unitrust Term Only

Trust Principal:	$500,000
Bypass of gains and charitable deduction:	$182,000
Annual income for 4 children for 10 years:	$50,000
After 10 years, charity receives:	$597,496

Charitable Remainder Retirement Unitrust

John Jones, 45; Mary Jones 45

Principal:	$200,000
Annual income after retirement:	$89,671
Charitable deduction tax benefit:	$21,150
Charity receives	>$1,000,000

Chapter 5

Annuities

"The habit of giving only enhances the desire to give."
Walt Whitman

Annuities Provide Security
~ *Fixed payments for life*
~*Rate is determined by age, up to 12%*
~ *Receive charitable deduction and*
tax-free income (portion)

THE FREEDOM OF CHOICE

If you are like me, you don't want anyone telling you what to do—especially your children. I met a man in China who was empowered by a gift of Heifer goats. He invited us into his home for tea and shared the customs of his country. He told us that at a certain age, especially in the poorer, more traditional families, the parenting role flip-flops, and the parents have to do what their children say.

This man had created a meaningful life with the goats he had been given. They provided nourishment and income for his family and fulfilled his dreams of a stable future for his children. When I met him I would guess he was about 70 years old, still a vital man. At that time, his son had come to him and said, "We're moving to the city." You see, his son had gone to school from the income of the goats and now was able to pursue his own career and choose how he wanted to live. The father, however, did not want to place the burden of his existence on his son.

He said lovingly, "You go. We'll be right here." Because of the goats, his son did not have to support him. He could pursue his career and build his own financial stability while his father could continue to support himself and live in the house he had built himself. He knew exactly how much he needed to live and exactly how much income his goats provided, year in and year out. And because the man was only responsible for himself—with his son on his own now and his wife passed—every new goat that was born was passed on to a neighbor, for free, because he had enough to provide for himself.

A Charitable Gift Annuity is much like those Heifer goats. It provides a dependable, fixed income for life and gives you the means to pass on more to others. It provides independence, security, and the freedom to choose how you want to live.

GIVEN FROM THE HEART

Jessie Mae Houston was small in stature, but her heart was as big as the world! She loved her family, her church, and Heifer. She lived her life in service to others, and she committed each day to making a difference.

Jessie Mae's first Gift Annuity of $10,000 was quite a stretch for her, but she wanted to do it because of her passion for helping the poor and hungry. Being a woman on a budget, she was pleased with the fact that she knew right away how much she would receive each year for the rest of her life. She was especially pleased that her original gift of $10,000 would go to Heifer upon her death. This assurance gave her peace of mind.

Jessie Mae was a busy woman with her grandchildren and church activities. She was not one to enjoy pouring over forms and applications. That's why she also liked the simplicity of carrying out the agreement of her gift. The application was easy to fill out, and she knew that her charity would provide her annual reports showing her the effect her gift would have on her taxes and deductions.

The Charitable Gift Annuity fit her needs to benefit her charity *and* retain income for herself. And soon she was funding more Gift Annuities each year. Finally, she took advantage of the opportunity to share her values with her grandchildren and created an annuity for each of them. In return, many of Jessie Mae's grandchildren have ceased to take the check and instead, they put the principal in an endowment honoring their Grandma. They learned their Grandmother's lessons of sharing and passing on the gift. They too wanted to help a world in need and recognize their grandmother for her generosity.

In total, Jessie Mae funded 38 Gift Annuities. When she died, the total value was over $100,000. She believed in the mission of Heifer and wanted to support it with a legacy.

A Chance to Give Back

Mrs. Kathryn Arnold recently celebrated her 102nd birthday. We communicate often, over the telephone and through letters, and she freely shares her faith and humor with me. She is no longer a strong woman, but she devotes her time to praying for others. "I may not be able to do too many things anymore," she says, "but I can still pray. That must do somebody some good or I wouldn't still be here."

Heifer has a special place in her heart. When she was a young girl, Kathryn lived with her parents in a three-room sod house on the prairie with a dirt floor and no indoor plumbing. The well was dug with a pick and shovel, and water was carried some distance in buckets. She attended a nine-grade, one-room Free Will School heated by a pot-bellied stove filled with coal, personally, by the school board. Every child in that school drank from the same dipper in the corner water bucket. Helping others lift themselves out of hunger and poverty is very important to Kathryn.

Kathryn and her now deceased husband, Arthur, learned about Heifer International when friends sent a contribution for a flock of chickens in the Arnold's name one Christmas. They were both so moved by Heifer's mission, they decided to arrange for an annuity that will help to support Kathryn after Arthur's death. After Kathryn passes, the remaining principal will be transferred to the Arthur and Kathryn Arnold Endowment Fund that was created as an ongoing celebration of the values by which the Arnolds lived and the many circles of giving they created.

THE GIFT OF SELF-WORTH

Ruby and Lamar Powell were introduced to Heifer in the '50s. In fact, Lamar was instrumental in influencing a group of farmers to provide one of the first heifers from the state of Arkansas for a project across the globe. From the beginning, both Ruby and Lamar recognized the value of the work of the organization. Ruby is spry and full of humor. She tells the story of how her husband rallied almost an entire state to donate heifers to the organization. She tells the story with such an obvious devotion for her now deceased husband, it's hard not to fall in love with him, too.

Lamar's career took them around the world on many adventures. They traveled and lived in foreign countries, always immersing themselves in the unique customs, smells, and landscapes of far-off places. They were captivated by the kindness and simplicity of the new friends they made wherever they went. While they enjoyed what each new place had to offer, they were haunted by the daily desperation, hunger, and poverty of the Third World countries they grew to know and love. They mourned for the children they saw digging through garbage, the homeless women who bathed at the public spigot, and the hungry people on almost every corner.

Years after Lamar and Ruby returned to the United States permanently, the plight of these people continued to haunt them both. They had donated small sums now and again to Heifer over the years, but they became reacquainted with the organization and fell in love with its mission all over again.

When Lamar died, Ruby began receiving a regular income from the Charitable Gift Annuity they set up through Heifer Foundation. She also volunteered for Heifer and continued to support specific projects that interested her. And boy, did she evangelize about its mission! It's hard to imagine Dan West doing a better job in the 1940s. She jokes that she became a "regular pain" when it came to talking about "her charity." She helped friends who couldn't think of what to get for their grandchildren's birthdays to consider buying a goat or rabbit in their beloveds' names. She volunteered at the local convention center and invited visitors to learn more about world hunger at one of Heifer's educational centers and global villages. She memorialized friends who died in recent years. Ruby did all of this because of her undying love for Heifer and Lamar. She feels that she honors Lamar and their shared values through her work of educating people about hunger and poverty.

According to Ruby, she's been blessed because she knows the divine joy of sharing. She also believes that is the basis for Heifer's success. She says, "Heifer gives people who had nothing the opportunity to give to others. Heifer is really giving self-worth."

THE BASICS ABOUT CHARITABLE GIFT ANNUITIES

Benefits of Annuities
~ *Regular, fixed payments for life*
~ *Payments that are as much or more than other financial arrangements*
~ *Generous tax benefits including income, capital gains, and estate taxes*

Charitable Gift Annuities, like Charitable Remainder Trusts, can be used for a variety of goals, such as providing for family or friends, or ensuring additional retirement income for yourself. But unlike a Charitable Remainder Trust, Gift Annuities are designed for people who want the security of a fixed payment sum, rather than a percentage of the principal of a trust property. And unlike commercial annuities, the remaining trust property goes to your charity at death.

How Charitable Gift Annuities Work

With a gift of cash or investments (not real estate), you and/or others receive fixed payments for life. The frequency and rate of payments are determined—and locked in—at the time the Gift Annuity is funded. The rate is determined by the industry standard, American Council of Gift Annuities, and is based on your age, or the age of your designated recipient. One of the attractive benefits of Charitable Gift Annuities is that payments continue for life.

When you establish an annuity, you will receive an immediate charitable income tax deduction for a portion of the gift amount. Also, a portion of the annual income you receive is tax-free for a number of years.

Gift Annuity Payments

Payments vary according to the age of the annuitant (person who receives the payment) at the time the annuity is funded. The older you are when you fund your gift annuity, the higher your payments will be. The rates below can give you an idea of payments, but an actual quote should be requested.

The amount of your Gift Annuity payments will never change. But the rate for each new annuity will be higher as you become older. For this reason, some—like Jessie Mae Houston above—choose to create a new annuity each year as part of their retirement planning. In this way, they make meaningful gifts over time while enjoying increasingly higher amounts of steady income.

For those who are looking forward to retirement, a Deferred Gift Annuity can be funded and invested today for payouts that begin after retirement.

TAX BENEFITS

A generous charitable income tax deduction is allowed for the year your Gift Annuity is funded. Capital gains tax that would be due on the sale of assets used to fund an annuity can be partially avoided with the remainder typically reported over the donor/annuitant's life expectancy. A Gift Annuity can be an excellent way to enjoy income tax savings today while ensuring that the amounts used to fund the annuity will never be subject to estate tax.

Enjoy Tax Savings

~ *A portion of the amount contributed for a gift annuity is deductible for federal income tax purposes*

~ *There can be additional income tax savings depending on your state of residence*

~ *Capital gains tax can be avoided or deferred when stock that has increased in value is used to fund a gift annuity*

~ *Gift annuity payments can be taxed more favorably than many other sources of income*

~ *Assets used to fund gift annuities are typically removed from your taxable estate*

~ *Gift or capital gains tax considerations may arise in some cases where a gift annuity is created for someone other than a spouse*

Calculating the Benefits of Your Gift Annuity

Average Gift Annuity Rates:

Age	Payout Rate
60	6.6%
70	7.9%
80	9.2%
90	12.0%

8.30% Gift Annuity

Mr. Jones, 76

Stock:	$50,000
Partial bypass of gain, save:	$3,316
Deduction:	$20,722
One life annual payout:	$4,150
Tax-free:	$496.76
Residual to charity:	$50,000

Deferred Gift Annuity

John Jones, 45; Mary Jones, 45

Gift:	$200,000
Bypass gain, save:	$45,005
Deduction:	$56,256
Two lives annual payout after retirement, partially tax-free:	$18,200
Residual to charity:	$200,000

Chapter 6

Endowments

*"It is every man's obligation to put back into the
world at least the equivalent of what he takes out of it."*
Albert Einstein

Endowments Feed the Heart
~ Choose a country or issue you would like to support
~ Honor a loved one
~ Create a legacy for future generations
~ Support Heifer programs worldwide

RED CONVERTIBLES

Peter and Joyce Branham aren't flashy. They lead simple lives in service to their community, and they're known for their generosity—donating time and money whenever possible.

Peter, however, suddenly developed an appreciation for his friend's convertible. He'd watch him drive down the street with the top down at that special time of year when the air feels pure and smells of cut grass, a time of year when the only place to be is outside. Boy, a convertible sure seemed nice, but it wasn't practical. Peter couldn't bring himself to spend that kind of money on such a luxury for himself. They didn't need a new car, much less a convertible. His wife agreed – no convertible.

As the summer kicked into full gear, Peter watched his friend drive by with the top down, wind ruffling his hair. It sure would be relaxing, he thought. But no, Peter told himself. No convertible.

As mid-summer approached, Joyce was out with some friends and ran into the bank to make a deposit. And there it was—this is true!—a raffle for a Red Mustang Convertible. Joyce filled out the contest form, stuck it in the box, and promptly forgot about it........ until the call came a few weeks later.

Wow! What a gift! Joyce and Peter picked up their new Mustang convertible at the dealer, and before going home, they drove everywhere they could think of, top down, waving to neighbors. When they got home, they parked the car in the driveway, got the lawn chairs out and just sat and admired that car, its beautiful color, the slick interior, that top that went up and down so easily. It was lovely, and the Branhams knew it was truly a gift from God.

They sat and watched that car until the shadows stretched long across the driveway. And then Joyce said,

"Peter, do we really need a new car?" You know how couples are together so long that they start to look a little bit alike? They start to finish each other's sentences, anticipate each other's needs, and read each other's minds?

When Joyce spoke, Peter had been thinking the same thing. How much good could the money for a car like that provide to the world? They had always given to others and found much joy in being selfless. How would they feel driving around in that car while others had nothing? They decided there was a special use for that car.

The Branhams have a particular love for orphans and want to make sure that these children never go to bed at night without knowing they are loved. Peter's father was an orphan, and their adopted son was an orphan. With the gift of the red convertible, the Branhams established the "Touch of Jesus Endowment for Orphans" through the Heifer Foundation to help orphaned children around the world. And they didn't stop with this one gift. Since they donated the car, they've given stock and other property to support their charity's work.

There are people in the world who receive lasting peace from helping others. The Branhams are among those people. Over time, the red paint of that convertible would have lost its luster, but their endowment continues to bless them and orphaned children around the world forever.

LIFE AFTER DEATH

Over the years, I have spent so much time becoming friends with donors. I have helped to build relationships that will last for generations. It's hard to describe what it's like to have the responsibility to ensure that all these wonderful peoples' desires are carried out. I am filled with feelings of joy, excitement, devotion, and of course sadness. The loss of caring donors and friends weighs heavy on my heart. Yet, I am honored to remember these people and honored to be able to help pass on their values.

My good friend, Lester Ford, knew his days were numbered when we met. He was an avid tennis lover. He had been a very good player at one time, but now he was living with Lou Gehrig's Disease, which had already progressed to the stage where walking was impossible. Planning for the future—the care of Lester's wife Mary and their four children, in particular —was not a luxury to the Fords. And caring for the future of those in need was a must. As a former investment banker, Lester was experienced and knowledgeable, in estate planning and charitable giving instruments. He knew his desires, and he wanted to make sure they were carried out in the present and after his death. He wanted to take care of Mary, his four sons, and then a world in great need. Everything he had devoted his life to.

After much discussion, a Charitable Remainder

Trust was set up to provide income for Mary and the four boys. While the family knew that the remainder of the trust would provide Heifer Foundation with a means to carry on the Ford's legacy of giving, they wanted to do more. So Lester and Mary also established the Ford Family Endowment.

While Lester and Mary began the endowment that day, it grew after Lester's death. During his memorial service, Mary, in her grief, shared the goals of the endowment with all of the people who loved Lester. She explained how much Lester wanted to continue to help others and how they could help carry out his wishes.

Today, Mary has turned the "fundraising" for their endowment over to the next generation. Her four sons are devoted to the memory of their father, and they share the values both their mother and father worked so hard to pass on.

Wisdom

My thoughts immediately turn to Hazel Mayfield when I think of wisdom. It's hard to adequately describe someone you love so intimately. Hazel was a guide for me, a second grandmother. Whenever she sent a card or letter, she always signed off with a heart. I met her in the fall of 1998, and I still carry her first letter with me. There have been many others since, each imparting more love, more wisdom, but her first is very special to me.

In that first letter, in just a few short sentences she reminded me of how important it is to always be kind, how important it is to never forget what is valuable in life, and how important it is to learn from each new situation we encounter. All of this was gracefully imparted in a six-sentence thank you note that she sent simply because I offered to drive her from her hotel to a Heifer meeting. From that point on, I had a mentor. I had a dear, dear friend. My first lesson of wisdom from Hazel was that the little things mean a lot...... a note, a ride, a hug.

Hazel served on Heifer Foundation's Board of Trustees. Her late husband Harold was one of the original Heifer cowboys who delivered livestock by boat to various countries. No doubt about it, the Mayfields knew how to be involved in charity work, and they were always a great resource for new ideas to raise awareness and support for their favorite causes. Hazel often said, "A little added to a little makes a lot." And she lived by that. Little notes, unexpected phone calls, tight hugs, and belly laughter all added up to big love.

I can remember our first brunch as if it were yesterday. I arrived at Hazel's home and was welcomed by an oversized American flag blowing with the cool breeze of that spring Sunday morning. Hazel told me that she put her flag out every day so that the neighbors would know she was up and feeling well. Another lesson: neighbors should care about neighbors.

She arrived at her door in a beautiful pink suit. She looked so elegant and business like all at the same time. She imparted wisdom just by being herself. I made a mental note to myself to always look my best. She invited me into her home, which was a perfect reflection of her personality – elegant. Hanging in the front entrance was a large antique mirror given to her by her parents. Her dining room table was set with Hazel's finest china and filled with pastry, fruit, meat, and assorted rolls. As we sat down for tea, I learned about Hazel's career in the insurance business and the difficulties she had in those days as a working woman. I realized how she and others like her paved the way for me to be in the position I was in.

Hazel also shared Harold's life with me. With a smile on her face and tears in her eyes, she shared his story. He founded his own brake business in the 1940s, and his reputation and passion for wheels landed him the thrill of his career—Indianapolis 500 mechanic! Harold was an avid traveler and together they visited dozens of countries around the world. He was a member of Palm Shrine #32, White Shrine of Jerusalem, and was a 50-year member of Union Lodge #58, F&AM, Scottish Rite Bodies, and Ben Ali Shrine. "He was the love of my life, and we had a ball," Hazel said. Tears ran down her cheeks. When she looked up and saw the tears in my eyes, she said, "Janet, we've now cried together, so we are indeed friends." She made me realize how lucky I am to have found my husband Randy. I shared her love story with my own daughters as they began to search for the right person to share their lives.

I then saw a glimpse into Hazel's charitable heart. She had given to charity for over 60 years. Her remarkable efforts to make a difference in the world touched her church, hospital, civic clubs, women groups, children organizations, and Heifer. I asked her how she was so moved, and she said, "Always listen to your donors and learn from what they have experienced and what they want to share with you. Wisdom is the key and you can only learn wisdom from experiences." Her gifts reflected a sense of ownership and partnership. She was sure that her gifts would make a positive difference to the charity— no matter what the size. "A little plus a little, makes a lot."

We finished our tea, and then we realized that hours had passed since we began our conversation. I thanked Hazel for sharing her heart, strength, encouragement, and wisdom with me. "I could not have shared it with you if you had not been willing to listen."

While nothing can replace a beloved friend or family member, her amazing wisdom and charitable heart lives on today. She established a memorial endowment for her husband, Harold, and after her own death, the Harold and Hazel Mayfield Memorial Endowment was funded with the residue of their estate. I miss her terribly, but I am reminded of her values and wisdom as I watch her endowment grow and help new families every year.

FAMILY LOVE

I know a woman who loves her in-laws dearly. I could end the story there, and it would be remarkable enough, but there's more. This woman had an opportunity to spend time in Guatemala, to visit with the people and see how they lived. She learned how important goats were to their livelihood; how these goats provide nourishment, income, and fertilizer for dry fields. She fell in love with the people of Guatemala, their customs and the countryside, and when she returned home, she shared all she saw with her husband. She asked him what he thought about starting an endowment in his parents' name to continue support in Guatemala. She loved her in-laws because of the generosity they always extended to her and others, and she wanted to honor them in a unique way.

At Christmas time, with all the presents under the tree and the entire family gathered, the son began to tell about Heifer International and how its work changes peoples' lives forever. He shared with his family that he and his wife created an endowment for Guatemala to honor them and their values. And it was an honor. His parents truly were honored to be given a gift of a legacy. To be told how their values had changed the lives of their children and would change lives in Guatemala forever.

A NEVER-ENDING LOVE STORY

Once upon a time, there lived a couple named Lawrence and Dorothy Goldman, who all their lives concerned themselves with meeting the needs of other people. Today, years after the Goldmans passed away, they are still embracing strangers in need across the globe, spreading their love and hope in Rwanda and Uganda. They did not have children, but during their 56 years of marriage, they befriended and guided many nieces and nephews and mentored other young people, especially medical students. Their lives were rich with friendships and travels.

The Goldmans lived simply, as was required by his modest salary and pension from the state hospital where he had served. They gave generously to help others. With their modest $700 savings in 1972, Dorothy bought 100 shares of Wal-Mart stock on the advice of a friend, who told her to never sell it. She didn't. They kept stuffing the certificates received from the stock splits, without counting them, into their bank lock box.

In 1993 when Dr. Goldman was diagnosed with cancer and struggled valiantly, he still attended public functions and Heifer events in his wheel chair. He was not afraid to die, but he did worry about whether his survivor's pension would be adequate for Mrs. Goldman. They visited a broker friend who advised them to put some of their stock into a charitable trust. By then, their 100 shares had multiplied to more than 70,000. They put 69,000 shares (then worth more than $1,000,000) into a charitable trust. After paying out 8% annually to the Goldmans, the trust assets were even greater at the end of their lifetime.

Heifer Foundation was only one of several beneficiaries of the Goldman's Charitable Remainder Trust. After both the Goldmans passed away, the portion of the trust designated for Heifer was used to establish a memorial endowment to benefit Heifer's work in Rwanda and Uganda. Every year, the endowment generates enough income to lift 25 families out of hunger and poverty.... every year! That's what we call a never-ending love story.

THE BASICS ABOUT ENDOWMENTS

Benefits of Endowments

~ *Create a family legacy of values*

~ *Provide an endless gift to the work of Heifer International*

~ *Designate your gifts for places and purposes that mean the most to you*

~ *Receive an immediate charitable deduction for tax purposes*

NAMED ENDOWMENTS

Donors are inspired in different ways by different people, issues, and places. That's why many want to give to their charities in a very personal way. By establishing an endowment that benefits a specific country, or brings awareness of, and hope to, people suffering from specific conditions or issues, you create an endless legacy of support that clearly states who and what is important to you. For generations to come, your family will know you by your values. And they too will have an opportunity to participate in what is so important to you, long after you've gone.

The example you provide to the world is so important that it should have a name on it. Named Endowments are a great way to eternalize a legacy of values. Many families choose to establish Named Endowments to honor traditions, mark achievements, or recognize their friends, relatives, or colleagues. Creating an endowment that bears your name makes a statement for future generations about the things that hold great importance in your life. Creating an endowment for someone else is a great way to make a lasting impression while saying "thank you" or "I love you" or marking special days such as birthdays, anniversaries and holidays.

MEMORIAL ENDOWMENTS

A Memorial Endowment is a wonderful way to create an ongoing legacy in memory of someone very special to you. Every year, loved ones will be reminded that those who have gone on were faithful to helping others in need. They were faithful to ending suffering around the world. A Memorial Endowment serves not only as a perennial source of income to your charity, it is also a continuing reminder of the values by which your loved one lived.

SPECIAL ENDOWMENTS

From AIDS awareness and prevention to the special needs of women and orphans, charities provide endowments to address the unique requirements of people around the world. We see so many people affected by war today — people who lived normal lives until war came into their community and destroyed their homes and hope — people who lost family members, a means for income, and a future. These people need our help to address the immediacy of hunger and homelessness as well as to help them build a future of security and prosperity.

We also see people affected by natural disasters – hurricanes, tornadoes, floods, and famine. These are people who need a new beginning and additional funds to rebuild their communities and respond to the threat of disease.

And there are women who struggle daily to do all the manual labor, provide all the needs of their children, cook and clean, and care for ailing parents — women without dignity — women who are beaten and abused by the men they live with. We must ensure these women are given the dignity and support that is so needed and so deserved.

With so many special endowments available, you can place your funds where your heart is, support the people you care about, and leave a legacy for loved ones.

Chapter 7

Wills, Living Trusts, and Bequests

"The future has a way of arriving unannounced."
George Will

It's Never Too Early to Have a Will or Living Trust
~ *Ensures property distribution according*
to your desires
~ *Protects family relationships*
~ *Minimizes attorney fees and court costs*
~ *Avoids unnecessary delays*
~ *Minimizes federal and state taxes*
~ *Ensures privacy for your family*

A WILL FOR PEACE

Ted and Adel Murray met while attending the same vacation Bible school in a small town in the rural Midwest. Both came from small family farms in neighboring townships within five miles of each other. Before long, they were attending the same school together and were married soon after graduation. There was a war, and then there were children.

Farming is what they knew, so farming is what they did. They raised corn, soybeans, and two bright, wonderful daughters. Ted took great pride in having grown up on a farm, raising his family on the same farm where he was reared, and providing for his family. In his community, a strong work ethic and providing for your family were the most important attributes a person could have. The couple made a decent living and had a wonderful life together.

Ted and Adel were able to give their daughters opportunities they had not had themselves. The girls went to college and soon had lives and families of their own. Careers took them to the big city, though, not back to the farm.

Over a lifetime of farming, the Murrays acquired a choice herd of cattle and highly coveted, rich, rolling, green farmland. For many years, their life together seemed to be picture-perfect. It was only days after celebrating his 70th birthday that Ted learned he had terminal cancer. He was devastated, not for his own sake, but, for the first time in his life, he feared that he would no longer be able to take care of his family. He was restless with anxiety about what the future would hold for his wife and family. It dawned on him that out of all the planning he had put into living, there was one thing he had failed to do for his family - he hadn't planned on dying. He didn't have a will or living trust.

I met the Murrays while giving a seminar in their community. After the seminar, the Murrays introduced themselves and invited me to their home for dinner. Ted had long been a supporter of Heifer International. Being a dairy farmer (and having been raised on a farm during the Great Depression), he, of all people, knew what one cow could do for a family. I visited with the Murrays and found out what their concerns and values were. Ted wanted to see that his family was cared for first, and then he wanted to help Heifer help others, as heifers had helped his family. After talking with him about his wishes and listening to his concerns, I was able to answer Mr. Murray's questions and provide him with the tools he needed to put his mind at ease. With the guidance of his attorney, Ted was able to put his estate in order.

A little over a year later, Ted passed away peacefully, knowing that he had taken care of his family *and* made provisions for families in parts of the world he would never know. His family shared with me the peace of mind this had given Ted in his final days. They also shared their gratitude for having been spared what many families go through during such a stressful time - when their loved one's wishes and legacy have not been adequately spelled out before their passing.

CARRYING OUT WISHES

I met Anna for the first time on a crisp fall day at a world hunger conference. Her husband of 56 years had just passed away that spring and she wanted to learn more about the organization he loved. Anna was a very petite woman and spent most of her life with books. She was a librarian and traveled the world by reading.

Wallace and Anna married right out of high school and built a life together. They led simple lives and were good stewards of their funds. They bought what they needed but not what they wanted because others did not have what they needed. They cared deeply about others.

After Wallace's passing, he left their $50 million estate to Anna. I had the honor of working with her to make sure that their estate would be distributed according to the desires and values that they had lived by.

Anna studied and compared many organizations before choosing Heifer Foundation to receive one-half of her estate and her congregation to receive the other half. Wallace's dedication to Heifer was very much a part of Anna's decisions, and it is the responsibility of Heifer Foundation to ensure the continued trust and integrity that he experienced with the organization.

THE BASICS ABOUT WILLS AND BEQUESTS

Seven out of ten people die without a will or any other estate planning document, such as a living trust. I read in a book about estate planning by a lawyer, Alexander Bove, Jr., that Abraham Lincoln died without a will. Pablo Picasso died without a will. And Howard Hughes died without a will—at least without one definitive will.

On the other hand, Alfred Bernhard Nobel immortalized his values through his will that established the Nobel Prizes. However, because Nobel wrote his will himself, without the help of professionals, long legal battles ensued, requiring the courts to clarify and interpret critical issues having to do with the selection of candidates and prize awards. After years of expensive proceedings in several different countries that were paid for by Nobel's estate, the remainder of the original estate went to carrying out Nobel's wishes—hopefully in the manner he intended.

Actually, everyone has an estate plan—whether you agreed to it or not. Every state provides laws that determine how your estate will be disposed of if you didn't make arrangements to do it yourself. In other words, if you don't have a valid will or living trust, the government will decide what to do with everything you worked so hard to build. And in many cases, a substantial portion of your assets could needlessly go to the government as estate taxes.

PROTECTING YOUR FAMILY

Has your family ever had a reunion? Isn't it amazing to listen to the old family stories when everyone is present? Ever notice how the story about Grandma and Grandpa's first meeting changes with each person's telling? Everyone's memory and perceptions are different.

When you have a will, you protect your family from different perceptions — from arguing over who knows best what you wanted. In their grief, each family member will want to do what's best, and chances are, each one has his or her own idea about what that is. Leaving a will or living trust is a gift to them. Your family won't have to guess about what was important to you. It will be clear.

Consider also those who depend on you for income. Dying without a will or other estate plan can cause probate and court delays that will delay your dependents from getting what they need. Your will states exactly what you want to happen, so those who rely on your support will benefit from your uninterrupted care, even after you're gone. You also want to protect your family's privacy. Establishing a living trust keeps your information and wishes within your family and out of the courts.

I have two lovely daughters and two wonderful sons-in-law. What do we, as parents, give to them? How do we make a difference in their lives by teaching them what good hard work will do for a person and what having all you want does for a person? Only you can decide what you are going to leave to your children. *If* you are going to leave something to your children. And if so, when do you want to give it to them—while you're still here to watch them enjoy your gifts? In a trust or as an outright gift? Those are the decisions only you can make. As an advisor once said, "Failing to plan is planning to fail." Planning now prevents problems later. And the good news is, wills and living trusts can be changed often and easily. New grandchildren are born. New friends are made. New passions are inspired. Your will or living trust represents your express wishes.

And what about your extended family? Your friends of 50 years; that cousin who was always like a brother to you? Without a will, your estate could go into probate, and only your immediate family will receive what's left of your life's work after taxes and expenses are taken out.

It's hard to plan for our own demise. It's emotional. There's also the perception that it's overwhelmingly time consuming and difficult to evaluate your options and prepare a will. Perhaps you think your estate is too small to worry about how it will be distributed. Or you're worried that it will cost too much in lawyer fees to prepare something now.

The truth is, not having a professionally-prepared estate plan can be more expensive to your estate in the end, and no estate is too small to distribute it in a way that will bring comfort to you and your loved ones. Your advisors and charities will help you through the process.

You will be at peace once you've decided how you want to pass on your valuables and values.

BEQUESTS

A bequest through your will or living trust can provide not only for your family and friends, but also for charitable organizations whose work is important to you. With a bequest you create a perpetual, living circle of giving. Many charities provide a number of options for you to consider. For example, at Heifer Foundation we automatically establish a permanent endowment named in your honor with your bequest—unless you indicate otherwise. You may, if you wish, designate how you want the income used, such as to support a particular part of the world, or for projects using a particular species of animal, for gender equality programs, or for education or general purposes. You can also designate that your bequest be spent immediately, rather than being invested in the Foundation's endowment. Your life. Your goals. Your plan.

VALUES TRANSFER

Your will clearly states your objectives. It transfers your values by example to your family and loved ones. It answers the question of what was important to you.

Do you have a house in the city? A condo in Florida and a bungalow in Maryland? A small apartment with some antiques and stock? What does your estate look like? There are only three places to distribute your wealth: family/friends, charity, and government. Good estate planning brings peace of mind to you and your loved ones. It brings gifts well beyond your possessions to those you care about.

It is never too early to get your estate in order. There is no age limit on when to begin preparing for your family's future, and there's no limit on how often you can change your will. By having a will or living trust, you gain peace of mind because you know that your family will be secure and your friends will know how much they were loved should something happen to you today. Including your charity in your estate plan shows your passion for a better world.

The right estate plan for you is one that if you were able to see the world after you're gone, you'd see a happy, financially sound family, and a world that is a far better place because of your values and valuables. The world is better because of the circle of giving you began.

Perhaps the greatest gift of Dan West's legacy is the requirement that recipients of Heifer animals pass on offspring to help another in need. Spreading success one family at a time throughout a community is a brilliant approach to creating a vibrant, economically equal, healthy region. But in truth, the real gift is an intangible blessing — a permanent change to the hearts and minds of people the world over. This is what the circle of giving is all about.

In all Heifer communities, passing on the gift of offspring is a celebration, a joyful event that is uniquely choreographed by each community, but universally recognized as momentous. When I was in China, I had the opportunity to witness a "Pass On" ceremony. It is one of the most exciting things that I've ever experienced. Ever!!

It took place in a small room with bare walls, several benches, and a desk. I had no idea what to expect. Would there be speeches? Would the ceremony be formal? And then it unfolded. From the back of the room a door opened and ten women entered. Each one was holding a basket full of beautiful, spotless white bunny rabbits. These women were full of excitement. Healthy laughter and teasing filled the small room. In their very movements I could see newfound dignity and spirit. These women were the joyful, confident hosts of an amazing party. With enormous smiles on their faces and a touch of pride in their carriage, they placed their ten full baskets down in front of the benches.

Then, behind them, ten women entered with empty baskets. These were much different women. They were frail and timid, respectful, yet watchful. They quickly set down their empty baskets and walked to the table where they began signing papers. I asked my guide what they were doing, and he told me that each recipient of a Heifer animal signs an official document that states they will pass on animals to a neighbor in need.

As the ceremony continued, we watched the full baskets become empty and the empty baskets become full. It was very hard for me to imagine that the women with the full baskets had at one time looked like the women receiving the bunnies. The difference between the two groups was so remarkable.

As the last basket was filled, there wasn't a dry eye in the house. Both sets of women were sobbing. Through a translator, I asked a woman who received a basket of bunnies why she was crying so hard. Isn't this a wonderful day? She was a tiny thing, thin with skin so pale, her veins were as visible as if they were on the surface. She kept her eyes lowered and said, "I now know what hope feels like."

Of course, I was crying too. And then I went up to a woman from the first group, a woman who struck me as the most playful and jolly. Again, through the translator I asked her why she was crying. And she said, "For the first time in my life, I know what it feels like to give something to someone. I never would have known how good it feels." The circle of giving feeds all its members.

You and I know what it feels like to give something to someone. Each of us has a full basket that we can empty every day: a neighbor next door or a friend in the hospital; a family in Kentucky who can't feed their children; a mother in Africa who is dying from AIDS; a stranger who needs a smile.

I believe it is our responsibility to give of all that we've been entrusted with—talents, time, valuables, and values. I know that together we can change lives. It is my endless joy to get to know donors; to hear their stories and learn what is important to each of them; to help them fulfill their hearts' desires.

Whether you support cancer research, youth-at-risk programs, your local police department, ending hunger and poverty, or your place of worship—whatever speaks to your heart—you create a living, breathing circle when you pass on your values through planned charitable giving. You help a world in much need, and you feed your own desire to make a difference.

Biography

Janet K. Ginn, CFRE is Heifer International Foundation's President, serving as its Chief Executive Officer. She leads the Foundation staff in three major areas: fundraising and education, gift administration and investment management.

Mrs. Ginn is a member of the International Board of Certified Fundraising Executives (CFRE) and is a graduate of Strategic Perspectives in Nonprofit Management at Harvard Business School. Mrs. Ginn is a Rotarian and holds memberships with the Financial Planning Association, Association of Fundraising Professionals, National Committee on Planned Giving, Arkansans for Charity Excellence and the Arkansas Council of Estate Planning. She also serves on the boards of the National Committee on Planned Giving Arkansas Council and Rotary Club 99 Foundation Board.

Mrs. Ginn is married to Randy Ginn, and they have two children: Shannon and Marsha. Shannon is married to Dale Connelly and they have one son, Isaac. Marsha is married to Brian Pierce.